Ready, set... write with CGP!

This CGP book is perfect for helping Year 3 pupils improve their writing — it's packed with guided activities based on a wide range of styles and genres, plus 'extra challenge' questions to get them writing independently.

Answers to every question are included in a cut-out-and-keep section, so it's easy to keep track of how pupils are getting on.

You can also download free annotated examples of a range of text types to give pupils ideas for their own writing. You'll find them here:

www.cgpbooks.co.uk/KS2WritingResources

What CGP is all about

Our sole aim here at CGP is to produce the highest quality books — carefully written, immaculately presented and dangerously close to being funny.

Then we work our socks off to get them out to you — at the cheapest possible prices.

Contents

The exercises in this book cover different types of writing, and different techniques you can use to make your writing effective. Use the contents below to see what's covered where.

Section 1 – Drafting Your Work

Section 2 – Writing Non-Fiction

Section 3 – Writing Fiction

Published by CGP

Editors: Claire Boulter, Andy Cashmore, Alex Fairer, Catherine Heygate, Katya Parkes, Hannah Roscoe

Contributors: Samantha Bensted, Alison Griffin, Amanda MacNaughton, Maxine Petrie

With thanks to Sean Walsh and Janet Berkeley for the proofreading.

With thanks to Emily Smith for the copyright research.

ISBN: 978 1 78294 954 1

Thumb illustration used throughout the book © iStock.com.

Images and clipart throughout the book from Corel® and clipart.com

Printed by Elanders Ltd, Newcastle upon Tyne.

Based on the classic CGP style created by Richard Parsons.

Planning Your Writing

Before you start writing, you need to plan your work — this includes thinking about the purpose and audience. The purpose and audience affect the language you use — e.g. a children's story might use descriptive and funny language.

Planning also includes thinking about how to structure your writing — e.g. how to start and end your text and what order your ideas should come in.

Key Terms

- **The purpose of a text is the reason why it's been written.** e.g. an advert to persuade the reader to buy something
- **The audience is the person or people who read a piece of writing.** e.g. a speech for teenagers, a letter to a friend

1 **These are extracts from different texts. Read the extracts and think about who the main audience for each text would be. Draw a line to match each extract to its main audience.**

The thief was last seen fleeing down Main Street, pursued by three courageous members of the public. Police are appealing for information.

I'm having a birthday party at mine and I'd love it if you could come! It's gonna be fab — hope you'll be there! Love and hugs, Maya

Once upon a time, there was a rabbit called Hopsy. Hopsy was a very naughty bunny. He was always in trouble with all the other rabbits.

A friend

Young children

Adults

2 **Circle the correct option from each pair of bold words to show the main purpose of each of these text ideas.**

A play script about a mission to space would **persuade** / **entertain** people.

Instructions for making raspberry jam would **inform** / **entertain** people.

A poster advertising for new members to join a choir would **entertain** / **persuade** people.

An explanation of the rules of basketball would **persuade** / **inform** people.

3 **This is the plan for a report on a class trip that will be put in the school newsletter. However, the points are in the wrong order. Number them from 1-5 to put them in the most sensible order.**

Conclusion ....

What you did after lunch ....

Introduction ....

What your favourite part of the day was ....

What happened when you arrived ....

Circle two pieces of information that should go in the introduction to this report.

Where you went on the trip

When you went on the trip

What time you got back to school

What you had for lunch

4 **A hotel owner is planning a leaflet to encourage people to stay at the hotel. Tick one feature the leaflet should include.**

Diagrams	☐	Persuasive language	✓
Informal language	☐	Rhyme	☐

Colour in two topics the hotel owner should cover in the leaflet.

Why other hotels are better	Details about the rooms ✓
Activities in the local area ✓	The terrible breakfasts

5 **Fill in the gaps to complete the plan for this story. Use the questions to help you.**

1. Beginning — Katie and her mum go to the cinema to see a film.

2. There's a problem — ....

....

....

3. But Katie has an idea — ....

....

....

4. End — ....

....

"I can plan fiction and non-fiction texts."

Editing Your Work

Every piece of writing you do needs to be edited. This means reading it carefully to check whether it makes sense and if you could make it better.

You can make your writing easier to read by removing unnecessary words, as well as by splitting or combining sentences.

Reading your work aloud can help you see how it could be improved.

1 These extracts are from a science fiction story. Put a tick next to the extracts that would be better if the sentences were combined.

1. The plant was in a large brown pot. It was in Dan's gran's greenhouse. ☐
2. Dan turned the key and slowly opened the door. He stepped into the greenhouse and immediately spotted the plant. ☑
3. The flower had deep red petals. The petals looked very soft. ☐

Put a tick next to the extracts that would be better if the sentences were split up.

4. The plant was snoring gently and Dan tiptoed closer so he could touch it. ☐
5. Suddenly, the plant moved. It saw Dan and licked its lips greedily. ☑
6. Dan yelled as the plant grabbed him and he tried to run but he couldn't. ☐

Choose one of the sentences you ticked and rewrite it to make it better.

Suddently, the giant plant moved Slowly. It saw Dan and ~~likked~~ licked his lips wildly.

Extra Challenge

Rewrite the other sentences you ticked.

2 **This is an extract from some instructions for making a pizza. Some of the words in the extract are repeated. Read the extract, then cross out any words that aren't needed.**

1. Use a knife to chop up the mushrooms and chop up the garlic.
2. Put some sauce onto the pizza base with a spoon and spread it around ~~with a spoon~~.
3. Sprinkle the cheese and sprinkle the toppings onto the pizza.
4. Put the pizza in the oven to bake for 30 minutes ~~in the oven.~~

3 **This is an extract from a story about an escaped rhino. Suggestions for how to improve it have been written in red. Read the extract, then read the suggestions.**

Split this first sentence into two shorter sentences.

The rhino crashed through the fence and snorted angrily and charged down the street towards the town square. When it reached the square, it stopped to take a drink from the fountain in the town square. After several moments, the rhino looked up. The rhino looked at all the people watching it from their windows.

These words aren't needed.

Combine these two sentences.

Rewrite the extract, using the suggestions to make it better.

T rhino crashed ~~throh~~ through the fence.

"I can edit my work to make it better."

Proofreading Your Work

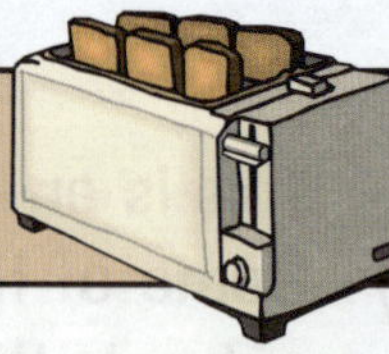

When you've finished editing your writing, you should proofread it. This means looking for mistakes in spelling, punctuation and grammar, as well as any places where the writing isn't clear.

1 **This is a late version of a newspaper article about a new invention. Read it carefully. Circle each mistake and write the correction above it. The first one has been done for you.**

There are 8 more mistakes for you to find in the text.

Scientist Invents Robot Toaster

an

The Toastinator 6000, created by Professor Carrie Kitson, is a incredible new robot toaster designed to make perfect toast every time

"The robot had all sorts of features," says Kitson. "It can butter the toast, add some jam and cut it up for you! Plus, you can ask the Toastinator to make you toast at specific times. it's great for anyone who's in a rush in the morning."

The Toastinator has been very popular with visitors at the annual Best Invention Competition, but Kitson admitts that there's still lots of testing to be done before people will be able to by one.

"As with any invetion, there are still some teething problems to iron out. For example, the robot sometimes throws toast at you and it blows raspberries if you dont put the bread in correctly.

"I can proofread my work and correct mistakes."

How to Make an Invisibility Potion

You need to write instructions clearly so that people can follow them.

You can use commands and prepositions to tell people exactly what they need to do and when.

Grammar Guide

- **Commands** are sentences that tell you to do something. They include a command word. — e.g. Add the chopped tomatoes.
- **Prepositions** tell you where or when something happens. — e.g. Soften the pasta sheets in hot water before assembling the lasagne.

1 **This is the start of a set of instructions for how to make an invisibility potion. Circle the command words.**

Where in each sentence is the command word? Why do you think that is?

1. Read the whole recipe before you begin.
2. Check that you have all the ingredients.
3. Mix the sea slime with the swamp juice.
4. Coat the inside of the cauldron with the mixture you have just made.

2 **Fill in the gaps to continue the instructions. Use command words from the box.**

5. ...Place... one hair from your head in the centre of the cauldron.
6. ...~~Bred~~ Break... a holly twig in half.
7. ...Drop... the twig halves into the cauldron.
8. ...Stir... five times in an anticlockwise direction.

~~Stir~~	Place	~~Break~~	Drop

3 **Unsuitable prepositions have been used in each of these sentences from the instructions. Rewrite each sentence with a suitable preposition.**

9. Mix powdered unicorn horn by dragon spit.

....

10. Spread this mixture above a mirror.

....

11. Place the mirror off the bottom of the cauldron.

....

12. Stir the potion during it turns blue.

....

Think about why it's important to use the right preposition when you write instructions.

4 **Use the pictures below to write the next three lines of the instructions. Include command words and prepositions.**

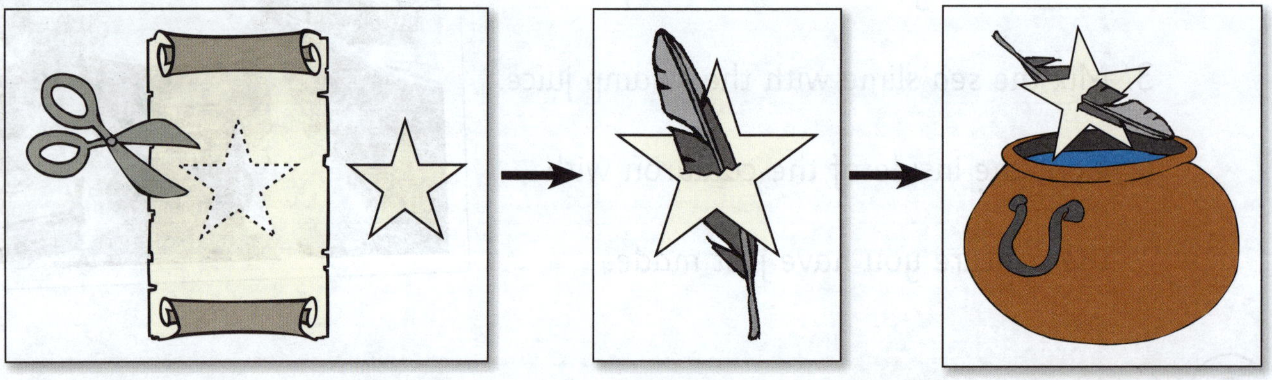

13. ....

....

14. ....

....

15. ....

....

Remember, commands tell the reader what to do and prepositions tell them where or when.

5 **Write the final three instructions for the potion. Use any of the command words, prepositions or ingredients in the boxes below, or come up with your own.**

16. ....

....

17. ....

....

18. ....

....

You could combine ingredients or take bits off one.

Think about how to get your new ingredients into the potion.

Your final step could be trying the potion.

melt chop roll place pour taste

in on into onto inside over

toadstool cobweb icicle leaf pebble

6 **Write instructions for making a jam sandwich. Use commands and prepositions.**

1. Place two slices of bread on a plate.
2. Spread ....
3. ....
4. ....
5. ....
6. Cut your sandwich in half.

"I can write clear instructions."

A Day at the Beach

When you write about something that you have done, you need to use the correct tenses so that your writing makes sense.

Use the past tense to write about events that happened in the past.
Use the present tense to write about how you feel about events now.

Key Terms

- The past tense is used to write about things that have already happened. e.g. I explored the woods with my friends and we made a den.
- The present tense is used to write about things that are happening now. e.g. I watch the dog as he chases his tail.

1. This is an extract from a diary entry about a day at the beach. Circle the words that are not in the correct tense, then write the correct word above them. The first one has been done for you.

Using the wrong tense makes it harder to understand the text. Think about why this is.

spent
Last week, I (spend) a day at the beach with my family. The sun was shining and there are no clouds in the sky. We buy ice creams and eat them as we walked towards the beach. I accidentally bump into my little sister and she dropped her ice cream. She cried until she goes bright red, and everyone stared at us.

Extra Challenge

Write a short paragraph about a day out that you have had recently. Use the past tense.

2 **Read this extract and circle the past tense option from each pair of bold words.**

Our dog Skye **bounded / bounds** towards the sea as soon as we **took / take** her off her lead. She **flings / flung** herself into the water and happily **swam / swims** around while we stood and laughed at her.

The sentences below are in the wrong tense. Rewrite each sentence in the correct tense.

Think about whether each event happened in the past or is happening at the moment.

Skye runs out and shakes water all over us.

....

She rolls in the sand and then digs a huge hole.

....

Even now, she still had sand in her fur.

....

3 **In the next extract, the writer describes bodyboarding. Fill in the gaps to complete the extract. Use the past tense form of the words in the box below.**

I pulled on my wetsuit, ... my bodyboard and .... into the sea. I .... a large wave approaching and .... very excited. I .... to kick just before it reached me. The wave picked me up and .... me towards the shore.

dash	see	grab	feel	begin	carry

The sentences below describe how the writer feels about bodyboarding now. Rewrite the sentences in the present tense.

Bodyboarding was my favourite hobby.

Bodyboardind is my favourite hobby.

I went bodyboarding whenever I could.

I am going to go bodyboarding when I can.

4 **Continue the diary entry. Write about getting back to the car, the journey home and how you feel now. Use tenses correctly.**

Remember to write in the first person, using words like 'I' and 'my'.

Use the past tense to write about what happened.

What was the walk back to the car like? How did you feel about leaving?

Did you stop for food or get stuck in a traffic jam on the way home?

Use the present tense to write about how you feel about the day now.

~~Not~~ Not long later, I had to go back home once we were aproching

Extra Challenge

Write a diary entry about your day. Make sure you use tenses correctly.

"I can use tenses correctly."

A Thank You Letter

Your writing will be easier to follow if it is **well-structured** — organising your writing into **paragraphs** will help to make the structure clear.

Using **statements** can help to make your writing more informative, while including some **questions** can help to keep your reader interested.

Key Terms

- **Paragraphs** are sections of writing that focus on a particular theme. You start a new paragraph when you start writing about a new time, place or topic. — e.g. All in all, this shows just how clever the plot of the film is.
  Another excellent thing about the film is the music.
- **A statement** tells the reader something. — e.g. Rowan can come out to play.
- **A question** asks the reader something. — e.g. Can Rowan come out to play?

1 These are sentences from a thank you letter. Draw a line to match each sentence to the correct paragraph topic.

Are you feeling better after your cold?	Thank aunt for birthday present
There was a giant balloon with my name on it.	Describe birthday party
I love the present you sent me.	Find out how aunt is
We had a magician who came and did tricks.	
I hope Uncle Stephen took good care of you.	

2 **This is the first paragraph of the letter. The writer wants to thank their aunt for the present and say how much they like it. Underline any sentences that don't fit the topic.**

When you've finished, read the extract again, skipping the sentences you underlined. Is it clearer? Why do you think this is?

Thank you for my birthday present. I have wanted a popcorn maker for ages. I also wanted a bike but I didn't get one. I've been watching loads of films just so I can eat popcorn. I sometimes eat chocolate when I watch films.

3 **This is the start of the second paragraph of the letter. The writer wants to describe the birthday party. Write three more statements about the party. Use the photo and the questions to help you.**

I really enjoyed my party. We played pass the parcel and I won.

What was the birthday cake like?

What other games were played?

What food was there?

....

....

....

....

....

....

....

4 **In the final paragraph of the letter, the writer wants to arrange for their aunt to visit. Fill in the gaps with questions — use the hints to help you.**

I really want to show you how the popcorn maker works.

Ask if she will visit. ....

I'm at a friend's party next weekend, but I'm free the weekend after that.

Find out when she is free. ....

5 **Write a thank you letter to a teacher or after-school club organiser who has helped you. Make sure each paragraph has a clear topic. Use statements to make the letter more informative. Use questions to interest the reader.**

Don't use too many questions — the letter should focus on thanking the reader and telling them what you're grateful for.

Dear ....

Thank you for ....

What did they help you with? ....

I really enjoyed ....

What did you enjoy most about what you did? You could ask what you will do next.

....

....

....

You were really good at helping me because ....

Was the person you're thanking very patient? Did they find a new way to help you learn something?

....

....

....

From ....

"I can organise my writing into paragraphs and use statements and questions correctly."

Amazing Alpacas

You need to make sure that your sentences follow on from one another. This will let the reader follow your points more easily.

You can use linking words to join your sentences.

Key Terms

Linking words join sentences together. Common linking words include: when, before, after, while, so, because.

e.g. The hamster was bored because his wheel was broken.
e.g. The hamster was pleased when his wheel was fixed.

1 **This is the introduction to a report about alpacas. Circle the correct option from each pair of linking words in bold.**

Try reading the text without the words in bold. Why do you think the writer included them?

Alpacas originally came from South America. They were first farmed for meat and wool around 6000 years ago, **after / before** they were bred from wild animals. Today, some people keep alpacas for their fleece, **when / while** others keep them as pets. They aren't common in Britain, **so / although** they are becoming more popular. More farmers now keep alpacas, **because / so** you might see one when you're next in the countryside.

Extra Challenge

Write four sentences about your pet or your favourite animal. Use these linking words to join the parts of each sentence: when, before, while, because.

2 This is the next part of the report. Fill in the gaps using linking words so that it flows and makes sense. You can use words from the box below or your own words.

Is It an Alpaca? Is It a Llama?

Alpaca

Alpacas are often confused with llamas .... they look quite similar. However, there are many differences between them. Alpacas have short, pointy ears, ... llamas have longer, banana-shaped ears. Llamas have coarser wool than alpacas, ... they look less fluffy. Llamas are much larger animals, ... alpacas can still grow to the size of a large deer.

Llama

so	while	before	although
because	when	after	

3 The three sentences below have been jumbled up. Draw lines to match the two halves of each sentence with the correct linking word.

Alpaca Wool

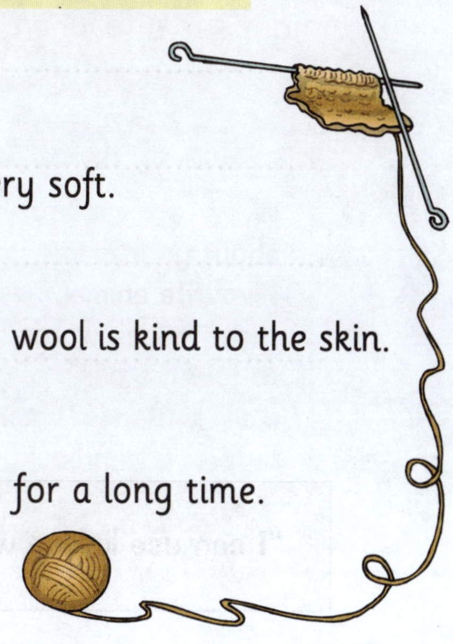

Alpaca wool is strong	because	it is very soft.
Alpaca wool is valuable	so	alpaca wool is kind to the skin.
Sheep's wool can be itchy	while	it lasts for a long time.

4 **Rewrite these pairs of sentences, using a linking word to join each pair.**

Owning and Looking After Alpacas

Alpacas get lonely. You need to own at least two.

....

Alpacas like hills. They're happy on flat land too.

....

Alpacas must be sheared. They can overheat.

....

5 **Rewrite the extract below, using linking words to join the sentences.**

Personality and Behaviour

Alpacas are curious. They are also shy. They are gentle and calm. People enjoy being around them. Alpacas are generally quiet animals. They sometimes make a humming sound. They are easy to train. They are very intelligent.

....

....

....

....

"I can use linking words to join sentences."

Classroom Cake Thief Strikes Again!

You can make your non-fiction writing clearer by breaking the text up into smaller chunks.

Layout features, such as headings and subheadings, can help to split up your text. The heading of a newspaper article is called a headline.

Key Terms

<u>Headings</u> and <u>headlines</u> tell the reader the main topic of the text.

e.g. 'Dinosaur Discovery' could be the headline of a newspaper report about finding a dinosaur fossil.

<u>Subheadings</u> divide up the text into smaller sections.

e.g. 'Accidental Find' could be the subheading of a section about how the fossil was found.

1 Read this headline from a newspaper article.
Explain what you think the article is going to be about.

<u>Classroom Cake Thief Strikes Again!</u>

....

....

....

....

....

....

Write another headline that could be used for this article.

A good headline is short, sums up the story and is interesting or funny.

....

2 **One of the following subheadings from the article does not sum up the section below it. Colour the box this subheading is in and write a better subheading for the section on the line below.**

Another Theft	**Outside**	**Not A Trace**
A cake thief has struck for the second time at Bray Primary School.	The cake was stolen when everyone was outside for a fire drill.	There were no clues about who had stolen the cake.

Subheadings should sum up the information in the section.

....

3 **This is an extract from the article. It should be split into three sections, each with a new subheading. Put a dash (/) in each place where the text should be split.**

Look for places where the topic changes.

Harry Alonso brought in a lemon cake yesterday morning. At around 11 am, Mr Cherry's pupils found that the cake had gone. Pupils in Mr Cherry's class make cakes when it is their birthday. They bring the cake in and share it. The first theft occurred two months ago. A pupil had brought in a cheesecake, which disappeared from the staffroom.

Extra Challenge

Write a subheading for each section you have marked.

4 **The sentences below are from the last two sections of the article. Write a subheading for each one.**

Subheading — ....

The pupil who brought the cake in was upset, and Mr Cherry was very angry.

Subheading — ....

Mr Cherry has come up with a plan to catch the thief red-handed.

5 **This is a later newspaper article, which reports the capture of the cake thief. Write the headline and subheadings for this article.**

Headline — ....

The classroom cake thief was caught in the act at Bray Primary School yesterday.

Subheading — ....

Mr Cherry left a plate of cakes on his desk under the eye of a hidden camera.

Subheading — ....

Bob, a bulldog owned by teacher Mrs Frost, was spotted gobbling up the cakes.

Subheading — ....

From now on, Bob will be confined to Mrs Frost's home during school hours.

Subheading — ....

Mrs Frost will bake a cake for every pupil's birthday as an apology.

Extra Challenge

Write an article about pupils cheating during the egg and spoon race on sports day. Use a headline and subheadings.

"I can use layout features to organise my writing."

Crime at Riddle Rock

Creating plot and characters is the starting point for any story.

Your plot needs to make sense and your characters should be interesting. You also need to make sure your characters fit into the plot you create.

Key Terms

The plot is made up of the main events of a story.	e.g. A girl goes to Mars to stop aliens invading Earth. She defeats them using X-Ray vision and saves the world.
Characters are the figures (normally people or animals) who feature in a story.	e.g. The main character in this story is an 8-year-old girl called Anika. She has X-Ray vision. Other characters include her pet rat, Bernard, and some evil aliens.

1. **Below is the plan for a detective character in a mystery story. Underline the options that make him an interesting character.**

Name: **Jamie / Detective Magnifico**

Personality: **Daring and quirky / Cautious and ordinary**

Unusual feature: **Red bow tie / Black hair**

Likes: **Tidying his room / Rock climbing with his pet fox**

Dislikes: **Vegetables / People making fun of his bow tie**

Write down one extra detail for this character that you feel will make him more interesting.

Does he have an exciting past, a funny catchphrase or a dark secret?

....

....

2 This is the plot of the mystery story. Fill in the gaps with interesting plot points. You can use the pictures and the prompts to help you.

The detective goes to Riddle Rock Castle to investigate ....

What is the crime? It could be a stolen pet. ....

At first, the detective suspects the cleaner because ....

What does the cleaner do that is suspicious? ....

Then the detective finds the vital clue: ....

Make sure the clue is related to the crime. ....

The chef confesses to the crime, saying she did it because ....

Why did the chef commit the crime? ....

3 Fill in the gaps to create an interesting chef character for the mystery story.

Name: Olivia / ~~chf~~ chef

Personality: angry/mad

Unusual feature: ....

Likes: ....

Dislikes: ....

Extra Detail: ....

....

4 Below is a story planning guide. Answer the questions to create a plot for a new story. Use one of the pictures to help you.

Make sure your plot makes sense.

Where does the story take place? ....

What does the main character have to do? ....

....

....

Why do they have to do this? ....

....

....

Who or what is stopping the main character? ....

....

....

How does the main character achieve their task? ....

....

....

....

Extra Challenge

Write a character sheet for the main character. Give them interesting characteristics and make sure they fit with the plot.

"I can create interesting plots and characters."

The Faraway Jungle

Every story needs to have a beginning, a middle and an end.

In the beginning, the characters and their goals are introduced. In the middle, the main events of the story happen. The end brings the story to a close. These parts have to be in this order so the reader can understand your story.

1. These are parts of several adventure stories. Draw a line from each beginning to a middle and then an end to create three adventure stories.

Beginning	Middle	End
Hazel crashes her plane in a jungle.	Hazel outwits a mean dinosaur.	Hazel leaves the jungle on a plane.
Hazel wakes up alone in a jungle.	Hazel finds a tribe who help her.	Hazel becomes the jungle's queen.
Hazel flies to a jungle to find monsters.	Hazel befriends two monkeys.	Hazel stays with her new friends.

Write a brief summary of one of the stories you created.

You can add extra details about what happens.

At the beginning, ...

....

....

....

....

....

....

2 **Below are parts of a different story that have been jumbled up. Next to each part, write whether it is the beginning, the middle or the end of the story.**

Hazel hides in a tree to escape. ....

Hazel sneaks past the crocodile while it sleeps. ....

Hazel is chased by a crocodile in the jungle. ....

3 **Below is the beginning and middle of another story. Write the end.**

Hazel touched down gently in the vast jungle clearing, her parachute trailing behind her. She looked around, eager to complete her mission.

Hazel took out a spade and began scraping the soil away carefully. After three hours of tedious digging, Hazel's arm ached and she wanted to give up.

Suddenly, something white poked through the soil. Hazel took out her brush and gently cleared away the soil. ....

....

....

....

....

4 **The photos below show a different adventure story. Write a story using the photos. Make sure your story has a beginning, a middle and an end.**

One day, Cameron was exploring the woods. He ....

What does Cameron plan to do in the woods? Is he looking for animals or searching for a cave?

After a while, Cameron decided to climb a tree. It was ....

Describe Cameron's climb and what he finds in the tree.

Cameron knew that he shouldn't touch the chick, so ....

What happens next? Does Cameron climb down? Does he see the mother bird return?

"I can write a story with a beginning, middle and end."

The Circus Comes to Town

You can make your writing more interesting by varying your sentence lengths.

Short sentences can help make your writing clear, and longer sentences can let you add detail or help your writing flow. Sentences and clauses can be joined together using linking words to make longer sentences.

Key Terms

- A clause is part of a sentence that has a verb and someone doing the action. e.g. Kelly stared at the new boy.
- Linking words join clauses or sentences together. e.g. Kelly stared at the new boy because he looked familiar.

1 **Read this extract from the beginning of a story about a trip to the circus.**

Ivan gazed wide-eyed at the huge circus tent and then he started sprinting as fast as he could towards it and he had forgotten that his mum was with him.

The sentence is too long, which makes it hard to follow. Rewrite the extract, splitting it into shorter sentences.

Look for linking words to help you decide where the extract should be split.

....

....

....

Read what you have written. Is it easier to read than the first extract? Why do you think this is?

2 These are six short sentences from the next part of the story. Draw a line from each sentence on the left to a linking word and then to a sentence on the right to make three longer sentences.

Make sure your longer sentences make sense.

Ivan's mum yelled.	so	She wanted Ivan to wait.
Ivan dashed into the tent.	because	She wasn't there.
He turned to speak to his mum.	but	He could get a good seat.

3 These sentences describe what Ivan sees inside the tent while looking for his mother. Add an extra clause to each sentence to make it more interesting.

A tall man breathed orange fire and ....

How did the audience react? ....

A clown filled a cannon with foam so..

What is the clown planning? ....

A nimble unicyclist changed direction suddenly because ....

Why did the unicyclist change direction? ....

Extra Challenge

Write three more sentences about different circus acts Ivan sees. Make sure each sentence has more than one clause and that the clauses are joined by a linking word.

4 **In the next part of the story, Ivan spots his mother. Rewrite this extract, joining some of the sentences together with linking words to help it flow.**

Ivan looked up. He saw his mum at one end of the tightrope. He wanted to get her attention. He waved. She didn't see. She was staring at the tightrope.

....

....

....

5 **Carry on the story by describing Ivan's mother crossing the tightrope. Use different sentence lengths to make your writing interesting.**

You could describe how anxious Ivan is, using short sentences to make his feelings clear.

Is Ivan's mother calm or nervous? Does anything happen while she is crossing the tightrope? You could use longer sentences to add detail.

....

....

....

....

....

....

Extra Challenge

Write the end of the story, where Ivan and his mother are reunited. Use different sentence lengths.

"I can vary my sentence lengths to make my writing interesting."

The Violinist and the Cowardly Cat

When you write a story, you need to describe the characters so they come alive in the reader's mind.

You can write interesting descriptions of characters by choosing your nouns, adjectives, verbs and adverbs carefully.

Grammar Guide

A noun is the name of something	e.g. the man
An adjective describes a noun	e.g. the tall man
A verb is a doing word	e.g. the tall man coughed
An adverb describes a verb	e.g. the tall man coughed loudly

1. **This is the start of a fairytale about a musician and his cat. For each pair of bold words, circle the option that makes the description more interesting.**

Once upon a time, there was a **nice / charming** musician called Danny who was always **beaming / smiling**. Danny didn't play his magical violin for money, but to make people **happy / joyful**. He took **good / excellent** care of his cat, Banjo, despite the fact that Banjo was scared of everything, including Danny's music. Every evening, Danny was **generous / kind** enough to share his dinner with Banjo.

(2) Rewrite these sentences about Banjo, replacing the verbs in bold to make them more interesting. Use the words in the box or choose your own.

★ Extra Challenge
Rewrite your new sentences, adding adverbs to them.

At night, Banjo **slept** with one eye open.

....

If he woke, he **looked** outside in case there was any danger.

....

One night, he **saw** a dark shape and **shook** with fear.

....

trembled	peek	dozed	gaze	glimpsed	slumbered	shivered	noticed

(3) In the next part of the story, an evil witch steals Danny's violin. Fill in the gaps with adverbs to show more clearly what the witch is like. Use the words in the box below or choose your own words.

The witch cackled .... as she spotted Banjo. She kicked .... at him, making him cower behind a pillow. As Danny stirred, the witch waved her wand .... at him, sending him into a deep sleep. She yanked the violin .... from his arms and grinned ....

viciously	slyly
violently	menacingly
expertly	forcefully
fiercely	cruelly
wickedly	wildly

(4) In this extract, some adjectives have been repeated, which makes it boring to read. Rewrite the extract, replacing the adjectives in bold to make it more interesting.

The witch looked **bad** and she smelt **bad**. **Dark** smoke billowed around her **dark** figure, which made Banjo feel **scared**. If he was going to get the violin back, Banjo couldn't be **scared**.

(5) Write the end of the story, in which Banjo defeats the witch and gets the violin back. Use interesting nouns, adjectives, verbs and adverbs.

You could use interesting adjectives to describe Banjo's bravery.

How does Banjo defeat the witch? With a cunning trick or a daring attack? What verbs could you use to describe it?

How does Banjo move? Does he stride confidently or tiptoe nervously? Use adverbs to add detail to your verbs.

"I can describe characters effectively."

The Time Traveller

When you write a story, you need to describe the setting so that readers can picture where things are happening.

You can write lifelike descriptions of places by choosing your nouns, adjectives, verbs and adverbs carefully.

Grammar Guide

- A noun is the name of something — e.g. the rain
- An adjective describes a noun — e.g. the cold rain
- A verb is a doing word — e.g. the cold rain poured
- An adverb describes a verb — e.g. the cold rain poured endlessly

1 This is an extract from a science fiction story about a time traveller. Read the text, then fill in the table to show what each description suggests about the setting.

Peter was immediately sweating. The grainy sand scorched his feet and the sun glared in his eyes. He hurried past a thirsty, wilting tree to a patch of shade that was being cast by a huge pyramid.

Example	What it shows about the setting
sweating	It is hot.
grainy sand	
the sun glared	
thirsty, wilting tree	

2 **Later in the story, Peter travels to the Ice Age. For each pair of bold verbs, circle the option that makes the description of the new setting more interesting.**

Peter shivered in the snowstorm that **swirled / moved** around him. The snow **was / lay** thick on the ground, and the wind **howled / blew** fiercely, **hitting / pelting** Peter's face with icy flakes. In the distance, he could see a herd of woolly mammoths **trudging / walking** towards him.

Think about which words give you a clearer picture of what's happening.

3 **Rewrite the sentences below, adding adjectives and adverbs to make them more interesting. Use the words in the box or choose your own words.**

The blizzard raged.

....

You can use adjectives, adverbs or both.

Chunks of ice floated on the lake.

....

Woolly mammoths stomped their feet.

....

Snow tumbled off the cliffs.

....

wildly freezing rapidly
violently furiously
gently mighty uneven
enormous powerful
jagged powdery tranquil

4 **In the next part of the story, Peter travels to the time of the dinosaurs. Fill in the gaps to describe the setting. Use the words in the box or choose your own.**

Hearing a loud .... above him, Peter dived under the shelter of a .... tree. He peered up and saw a group of pterodactyls gliding .... through the .... sky. They eyed the .... fish that were .... upstream.

lush	squawk	clear	majestically	drifting	screech
gracefully	leafy	silver	slender	darting	cloudless

5 **Continue the story by describing the setting in the picture. Use interesting nouns, adjectives, verbs and adverbs.**

....

....

....

....

....

....

....

....

....

....

"I can describe settings effectively."

Ridiculous Rhymes

Poems are creative pieces of writing which often use lots of description and rhyme. Rhyming is a great way to make poems funny. You can also add more humour to poems by using nonsense words.

Key Terms

- **Words rhyme if they end with the same sound.** — e.g. The other night I had a dream,
That I found a tiny stream.
- **A nonsense word is a made-up word with no accepted meaning.** — e.g. There I saw a flumberfloose,
With antlers like a mighty moose.

1 **This is part of a poem about an adventure at sea. Read the extract, then circle all the words that rhyme.**

I saw a shark with pointy teeth;

It swam to my boat and dived underneath.

Its skin was smooth and blueish grey,

And it surfed the waves on that sunny day.

I watched it leap out of the sea,

And as it turned, it grinned at me.

"How strange!" I cried, when it had gone.

"It was as graceful as a swan."

In a shape poem, the words are arranged in the same shape as the topic of the poem. If the extract above was a shape poem, what shape would it be?

....

Extra Challenge

Write a shape poem about your favourite animal. It doesn't have to rhyme.

2 **This is an extract from another poem. Fill in the gaps with your own rhymes. Make them as funny as you like.**

In this extract, the first two lines should rhyme, and so should the last two.

I met a big grey elephant, sitting in a .... ,

He waved his trunk and flapped his ears, and he said to .... ,

"I know I'm odd just sitting here, staring at the .... ,

"But I'm happy in my tree because it's always ...."

★ Extra Challenge

Write the next four lines in the poem. Make sure each pair of lines rhymes.

3 **Nonsense poems are about imaginary places or situations. They often use lots of nonsense words. Read this extract from a nonsense poem, then complete the task below.**

A nonsense word is a made-up word with no accepted meaning.

Far away in Dangledoo there is a clump of trees,

Whose leaves are red with purple spots and pockets full of cheese.

There you'll find the bundywee with its giant snooses,

Who feasts upon the pomblefruit and its tasty juices.

Let's not forget the sassaloo, who slithers on the floor,

Or the tiny hinkersnatch, who has a mighty snore.

Underline all the nonsense words in the extract. Choose your favourite nonsense word and draw what you think it's describing in the box.

4 **Free verse is a type of poetry that doesn't follow any rules. The words don't have to rhyme and the lines can be any length. Read the extract below, then write the next three lines. Try to add some humour to the poem.**

I made some monsters out of meatballs;

They have carrot noses and onion eyebrows,

And I used some parsley for their hair.

They're angry because I'm going to eat them.

I know they'll be delicious.

First, I'll eat their pasta blankets.

....

....

....

Extra Challenge

Write a free verse poem about your favourite food.

5 **Write a short poem about a wizard. Use rhymes and nonsense words to make it as funny as possible.**

Hint: words like head and hat have lots of rhymes.

There was a wizard from the west,

....

....

....

Is the wizard good or bad at magic?

You could make up nonsense words for the wizard's spells.

....

....

"I can make my poems funny by using rhymes and nonsense words."

Answers

Pages 3-5 — Planning Your Writing

1. You should have matched the extracts like this:
   Extract 1 — Adults
   Extract 2 — A friend
   Extract 3 — Young children
2. You should have circled the words in bold:
   - A play script about a mission to space would **entertain** people.
   - Instructions for making raspberry jam would **inform** people.
   - A poster advertising for new members to join a choir would **persuade** people.
   - An explanation of the rules of basketball would **inform** people.
3. You should have labelled the points like this:
   - Conclusion — **5**
   - What you did after lunch — **3**
   - Introduction — **1**
   - What your favourite part of the day was — **4**
   - What happened when you arrived — **2**

   You should have circled:
   - Where you went on the trip
   - When you went on the trip
4. You should have ticked:
   - Persuasive language

   You should have coloured:
   - Activities in the local area
   - Details about the rooms
5. Any suitable plan for the story. For example:
   1. Beginning — Katie goes to the cinema with her mum to see a long-awaited film.
   2. There's a problem — the film is so popular that there are no tickets left.
   3. But Katie has an idea — she sees a sign for a bowling competition and suggests they go there instead.
   4. End — they enjoy the bowling and win tickets to see the film the next day.

Pages 6-7 — Editing Your Work

1. You should have ticked sentences 1, 3, 4 and 6.
   Any suitable rewriting of your chosen sentence. For example:
   - The plant was in a large brown pot in Dan's gran's greenhouse.
   - The flower had deep red petals which looked very soft.
   - The plant was snoring gently. Dan tiptoed closer so he could touch it.
   - Dan yelled as the plant grabbed him. He tried to run but he couldn't.
2. You should have crossed out unnecessary words to avoid repetition. For example:
   - Use a knife to chop up the mushrooms and ~~chop up~~ the garlic.
   - Put some tomato sauce onto the pizza base with a spoon and spread it around ~~with a spoon~~.
   - Sprinkle the cheese and ~~sprinkle~~ the toppings onto the pizza.
   - Put the pizza in the oven to bake for 30 minutes ~~in the oven~~.
3. Any suitable rewriting that uses the suggestions to make the extract better. For example:
   The rhino crashed through the fence and snorted angrily. It charged down the street towards the town square. When it reached the square, it stopped to take a drink from the fountain. After several moments, the rhino looked up at all the people watching it from their windows.

Answers

Page 8 — Proofreading Your Work

1. These are the errors you should have marked and corrected in the text:

   Scientist Invents Robot Toaster

   The Toastinator 6000, created by Professor Carrie Kitson, is a (an) incredible new robot toaster designed to make perfect toast every time(.)

   "The robot **had (has)** all sorts of features," says Kitson. "It can butter the toast, add some jam and cut it up for you! Plus, you can ask the Toastinator to make you toast at specific times. **it's (It's)** great for anyone who's in a rush in the morning."

   The Toastinator has been very popular with visitors at the annual Best Invention Competition, but Kitson **admitts (admits)** that there's still lots of testing to be done before people will be able to **by (buy)** one.

   "As with any **invetion (invention)**, there are still some teething problems to iron out. For example, the robot sometimes throws toast at you and it blows raspberries if you **dont (don't)** put the bread in correctly.**(")**

Pages 9-11 — How to Make an Invisibility Potion

1. You should have circled:
   Read, Check, Mix, Coat
2. You should have filled the gaps like this:
   Place one hair from your head in the centre of the cauldron.
   Break a holly twig in half
   Drop the twig halves into the cauldron.
   Stir five times in an anticlockwise direction.
3. Any suitable prepositions. For example:
   Mix powdered unicorn horn **with** dragon spit.
   Spread this mixture **across** a mirror.
   Place the mirror **in** the bottom of the cauldron.
   Stir the potion **until** it turns blue.
4. Any suitable instructions which use command words and prepositions. For example:
   Cut a large star **out of** a piece of parchment.
   Push a feather **through** the middle of the star.
   Drop the star and feather **into** the cauldron.
5. Any suitable instructions which use command words and prepositions. For example:
   Place a cobweb **on** the surface of the potion.
   Melt an icicle **over** the cobweb.
   Pour some of the potion **into** a cup and **taste** it.
6. Your instructions should use commands and prepositions so they are easy to follow.
   For example:
   2. **Spread** butter **onto** both slices of bread.
   3. **Dollop** jam **on** one slice of the bread.
   4. **Spread** the jam evenly **across** the bread.
   5. Put one slice of bread **on top of** the other.

Pages 12-14 — A Day at the Beach

1. These are the errors you should have marked and corrected:

   Last week, I spend (spent) a day at the beach with my family. The sun was shining and there are **(were)** no clouds in the sky. We buy **(bought)** ice creams and eat **(ate)** them as we walked towards the beach. I accidentally bump **(bumped)** into my little sister and she dropped her ice cream. She cried until she goes **(went)** bright red, and everyone stared at us.
2. You should have circled the words in bold:

   Our dog Skye **bounded** towards the sea as soon as we **took** her off her lead. She **flung** herself into the water and happily **swam** around while we stood and laughed at her.

   Any suitable rewriting of the sentences that uses the correct tense. For example:
   - Skye **ran** out and **shook** water all over us.
   - She **rolled** in the sand and then **dug** a huge hole.
   - Even now, she still **has** sand in her fur.
3. You should have filled in the gaps like this:

   I pulled on my wetsuit, **grabbed** my bodyboard and **dashed** into the sea. I **saw** a large wave approaching and **felt** very excited. I **began** to kick just before it reached me. The wave picked me up and **carried** me towards the shore.

Answers

Any suitable rewriting of the sentences which uses the present tense. For example:

- Bodyboarding is my favourite hobby.
- I go bodyboarding whenever I can.

4. Your diary entry should use the past and present tenses correctly. Here are some techniques you should have used:
   - You should have used the past tense to write about what happened, e.g. 'We **packed** away our things, but I **didn't** want to leave. I **dragged** my feet as we **walked** back to the car.'
   - You should have used the present tense to write about how you feel now, e.g. 'I still **think** about our fun day out. The beach **is** one of my favourite places to visit.'

Pages 15-17 — A Thank You Letter

1. You should have joined the sentences to the topics like this:

   Are you feeling better after your cold? — Find out how aunt is

   There was a giant balloon with my name on it. — Describe birthday party

   I love the present you sent me. — Thank aunt for birthday present

   We had a magician who came and did tricks. — Describe birthday party

   I hope Uncle Stephen took good care of you. — Find out how aunt is
2. You should have underlined these sentences:

   I also wanted a bike but I didn't get one.
   I sometimes eat chocolate when I watch films.
3. Any three suitable statements about the birthday party. For example:

   We played hide and seek in the garden. Dad cooked tasty burgers on the barbecue. Dad baked me a delicious birthday cake that was shaped like a penguin.
4. Any suitable questions that fit with the paragraph topic. For example:

   In the first gap:

   Please will you come and visit soon?

   In the second gap:

   Are you free on that weekend?
5. You should have written a thank you letter. Here are some techniques you could have used:
   - Paragraphs with separate topics, e.g. First paragraph thanking your guitar teacher for helping you learn to play a difficult piece of music. Second paragraph saying you enjoyed learning new chords most. Third paragraph telling your teacher they were good at helping because they were very patient, and asking them what music they like to play on the guitar.
   - Statements to show what you enjoyed about the help you received, e.g. 'I really enjoyed being able to play the new chords because it meant that I could play my favourite song.'
   - Questions to interest your reader, e.g. 'What will we be learning next week?'

Pages 18-20 — Amazing Alpacas

1. You should have circled the words in bold:
   Alpacas originally came from South America. They were first farmed for meat and wool around 6000 years ago, **after** they were bred from wild animals. Today, some people keep alpacas for their fleece, **while** others keep them as pets. They aren't common in Britain, **although** they are becoming more popular. More farmers now keep alpacas, **so** you might see one when you're next in the countryside.
2. Any suitable linking words. For example:
   Alpacas are often confused with llamas **because** they look quite similar. However, there are many differences between them. Alpacas have short, pointy ears, **while** llamas have longer, banana-shaped ears. Llamas have coarser wool than alpacas, **so** they look less fluffy. Llamas are much larger animals, **although** alpacas can still grow to the size of a large deer.
3. You should have matched up:

   Alpaca wool is strong — so — it lasts for a long time.

   Alpaca wool is valuable — because — it is very soft.

   Sheep's wool can be itchy — while — alpaca wool is kind to the skin.

Answers

4. Any suitable rewriting of the sentences using linking words. For example:

   Alpacas get lonely **so** you need to own at least two.

   Alpacas like hills **but** they're happy on flat land too.

   Alpacas must be sheared **because** they can overheat.

5. You should have rewritten the extract using sensible linking words to join the sentences. For example:

   Alpacas are curious, **but** they are also shy. They are gentle and calm, **so** people enjoy being around them. Alpacas are generally quiet animals, **although** they sometimes make a humming sound. They are easy to train **because** they are very intelligent.

Pages 21-23 — Classroom Cake Thief Strikes Again!

1. Any suitable summary which matches the headline. For example:

   The article will be about a thief who has stolen a cake from a school. The thief has stolen cake from the school before.

   You should have written a different headline. For example:

   'Another Cake Swiped From School' / 'Cake Theft Causes Classroom Tears'

2. You should have coloured the second box.

   Any suitable subheading, e.g. 'The Perfect Distraction' / 'Pupils Outside When Thief Strikes'

3. You should have added a dash (/) in the following places:

   Harry Alonso brought in a lemon cake yesterday morning. At around 11 am, Mr Cherry's pupils found that the cake had gone. / Pupils in Mr Cherry's class make cakes when it is their birthday. They bring the cake in and share it. / The first theft occurred two months ago. A pupil had brought in a cheesecake, which disappeared from the staffroom.

4. Any suitable suggestions for subheadings. For example:

   For the first section — 'Pupil Heartbroken' / 'Teacher's Rage at Theft'

   For the second section — 'On The Case' / 'Teacher's Plan'

5. You should have written a headline and subheadings that match the sentences in the article. Here are some techniques you could have used:

   - An interesting headline that sums up the article, e.g. 'Cake Thief Caught on Camera!'
   - Short subheadings that show what the following sections are about, e.g. 'Setting the Trap', 'Cunning Canine', 'In the Doghouse', 'Teacher Makes Amends'.

Pages 24-26 — Crime at Riddle Rock

1. You should have circled the following:

   Detective Magnifico, Daring and quirky, Red bow tie, Rock climbing with his pet fox, People making fun of his bow tie

   Any interesting extra detail that adds to his character. For example:

   He became a detective to find his missing sister.

2. Any suitable points that create a plot which makes sense. For example:

   The detective goes to Riddle Rock Castle to investigate **a stolen dog.** At first, the detective suspects the cleaner because **she won't answer any questions about the dog**. Then the detective finds the vital clue: **paw prints on the kitchen floor**. The chef confesses to the crime, saying she did it because **the dog is a good chef and she wanted it to do all the cooking**.

3. Any interesting characteristics that fit the mystery story. For example:

   Name: Chef Burntoast

   Personality: Angry and greedy

   Unusual Feature: Golden rolling pin

   Likes: Making mashed potato sculptures

   Dislikes: Cooking difficult dishes

   Extra Detail: She keeps a spare spatula underneath her chef's hat.

Answers

4. Any suitable plot that is interesting and makes sense. You should have included:
   - A suitable location, e.g. 'On a glacier in Antarctica.'
   - An interesting task for the main character, e.g. 'She has to reach a hidden cave on the far side of the glacier.'
   - A reason for the main character's actions that fits with what they have to do, e.g. 'She has to do this because her pet seal, Lewis, is stuck in a deep pool in the cave.'
   - An interesting problem or villain for the main character to overcome, e.g. 'An avalanche stops her from getting into the cave.'
   - A suitable way for the main character to overcome the problem or villain they face, e.g. 'She digs her way through the avalanche, and rescues Lewis. They go home together.'

Pages 27-29 — The Faraway Jungle

1. Any combination of a beginning, a middle and an end that creates a logical story. For example:

   Hazel crashes her plane in a jungle. — Hazel finds a tribe who help her. — Hazel leaves the jungle on a plane.

   Hazel wakes up alone in a jungle. — Hazel befriends two monkeys. — Hazel stays with her new friends.

   Hazel flies to a jungle to find monsters. — Hazel outwits a mean dinosaur. — Hazel becomes the jungle's queen.

   You should have written a summary of one of the stories. For example:

   At the beginning, Hazel crashes her plane in a jungle after a wing falls off. She travels through the jungle and meets a friendly tribe. They provide her with wood so she can build a makeshift wing. She leaves the jungle on her plane.
2. You should have labelled the first sentence as 'middle', the second sentence as 'end' and the first sentence as 'beginning'.
3. You should have written an ending that brings the story to a close. For example:

   She imagined that this was the new species of dinosaur that she had been seeking. Then, as she brushed more soil aside, she groaned. It was just a plastic bag. Dripping in sweat and covered in dirt, Hazel decided to go home and try again tomorrow.
4. You should have written a story with a clear beginning, middle and end. Here is a structure you could have used:
   - A beginning that introduces Cameron, e.g. 'He loved spending time in the woods, watching the animals that lived there. His favourites were the birds that flitted between the trees.'
   - A middle that shows Cameron climbing the tree and coming across the chick, e.g. 'It was hard work. His muscles ached by the time he reached the top, but it was worth it because he could see the whole forest. Suddenly, Cameron heard a cheep and spotted a fluffy brown chick in a nest nearby.'
   - An end that brings the story to a close, e.g. 'Cameron knew that he shouldn't touch the chick, so he scrambled back down the tree. Just then, the mother bird glided into the nest with a worm for the chick. Cameron went home to tell his mum about his adventure.'

Pages 30-32 — The Circus Comes to Town

1. You should have split the extract into shorter sentences. For example:

   Ivan gazed wide-eyed at the huge circus tent. He started sprinting as fast as he could towards it. He had forgotten that his mum was with him.
2. You should have joined the sentences like this:

   Ivan's mum yelled. — because — She wanted Ivan to wait.

   Ivan dashed into the tent. — so — He could get a good seat.

   He turned to speak to his mum. — but — She wasn't there.

Answers

3. Any suitable clauses that follow on from the start of the sentence. For example:
    - A tall man breathed orange fire and the audience applauded excitedly.
    - A clown filled a cannon with foam so he could fire it at the ringmaster.
    - A nimble unicyclist changed direction suddenly because a clown car rolled in front of her.
4. Any suitable rewriting of the extract which joins the short sentences together. For example:
   Ivan looked up **and** he saw his mum at one end of the tightrope. He wanted to get her attention **so** he waved. She didn't see **because** she was staring at the tightrope.
5. You should have described Ivan's mother crossing the tightrope. Here are some techniques you could have used:
    - Short sentences to make it clear how anxious Ivan is, e.g. 'Ivan's heart raced. His stomach hurt. He didn't want his mother to fall.'
    - Long sentences to add detail, e.g. 'Ivan's mother spread her arms out wide so she could keep her balance as she stepped along the tightrope.'
    - A variety of sentence lengths, e.g. 'She stopped halfway and wobbled from side to side. The audience gasped fearfully. Ivan covered his eyes.'

Pages 33-35 — The Violinist and the Cowardly Cat

1. You should have circled the words in bold:
   Once upon a time, there was a **charming** musician called Danny who was always **beaming**. Danny didn't play his magical violin for money, but to make people **joyful**. He took **excellent** care of his cat, Banjo, despite the fact that Banjo was scared of everything, including Danny's music. Every evening, Danny was **generous** enough to share his dinner with Banjo.
2. Any suitable sentences that use a more interesting verb. For example:
    - At night, Banjo **dozed** with one eye open.
    - If he woke, he **peeked** outside in case there was any danger.
    - One night, he **glimpsed** a dark shape and **trembled** with fear.
3. Any suitable adverbs. For example:
   The witch cackled **wickedly** as she spotted Banjo. She kicked **viciously** at him, making him cower behind a pillow. As Danny stirred, the witch waved her wand **expertly** at him, sending him into a deep sleep. She yanked the violin **forcefully** from his arms and grinned **cruelly**.
4. You should have rewritten the extract, replacing the adjectives in bold with more interesting adjectives. For example:
   The witch looked **sinister** and she smelt **vile**. **Murky** smoke billowed around her **shadowy** figure, which made Banjo feel **anxious**. If he was going to get the violin back, Banjo couldn't be **frightened**.
5. You should have written an ending which describes Banjo defeating the witch. Here are some techniques you could have used:
    - Striking adjectives to describe Banjo being brave, e.g. 'Banjo's **powerful** roar made the **wicked** witch tremble.'
    - Interesting verbs to describe Banjo's fight with the witch, e.g. 'Banjo **leapt** at the witch and **snatched** her wand between his teeth.'
    - Adverbs to describe the witch's actions as she is defeated, e.g. 'As the spell hit her, the witch slumped **heavily** to the ground and started snoring **deafeningly**.'

Pages 36-38 — The Time Traveller

1. Any suitable suggestions for what each example shows about the setting. For example:

Example	What it shows about the setting
sweating	It is hot.
grainy sand	The setting could be a desert.
the sun glared	The sun is strong and bright.
thirsty, wilting tree	It is very dry.

Answers

2. You should have circled the words in bold:
   Peter shivered in the snowstorm that **swirled** around him. The snow **lay** thick on the ground, and the wind **howled** fiercely, **pelting** Peter's face with icy flakes. In the distance, he could see a herd of woolly mammoths **trudging** towards him.
3. You should have rewritten the sentences with adjectives, adverbs or both. For example:
   - The **powerful** blizzard raged **furiously**.
   - **Jagged** chunks of ice floated **gently** on the **tranquil** lake.
   - **Enormous** woolly mammoths stomped their **mighty** feet **wildly**.
   - **Powdery** snow tumbled **rapidly** off the **uneven** cliffs.
4. Any suitable words. For example:
   Hearing a loud **screech** above him, Peter dived under the shelter of a **leafy** tree. He peered up and saw a group of pterodactyls gliding **gracefully** through the **cloudless** sky. They eyed the **slender** fish that were **darting** upstream.
5. You should have continued the story by describing the setting. Here are some techniques you could have used:
   - Nouns and adjectives to describe the landscape, e.g. 'A **roaring waterfall** threw up **clouds** of **shimmering spray**.'
   - Verbs to describe the actions of the dinosaurs, e.g. 'The long-necked dinosaurs **sloshed** through the clear water, **pausing** to **slurp** huge mouthfuls.'
   - Adverbs to make your verbs interesting, e.g. 'The dinosaurs tugged **forcefully** on the juicy leaves, chewing **noisily** as they ate.'

Pages 39-41 — Ridiculous Rhymes

1. You should have circled:
   teeth, underneath, grey, day, sea, me, gone, swan
   You should have written:
   It would be in the shape of a shark.
2. Any suitable pairs of words that rhyme.
   For example:
   I met a big grey elephant, sitting in a **tree**,
   He waved his trunk and flapped his ears, and he said to **me**.
   "I know I'm odd just sitting here, staring at the **sky**,
   "But I'm happy in my tree because it's always **dry**."
3. You should have underlined these words:
   Dangledoo, bundywee, snooses, pomblefruit, sassaloo, hinkersnatch
   Any drawing of a nonsense creature or object mentioned in the poem.
4. Any suitable sentences that continue the poem. For example:
   Then I'll dip each meatball in tomato sauce;
   It'll look like they're wearing red skirts!
   I'll make them some shoes out of lettuce.
5. Your poem should include rhymes and nonsense words to make it funny. For example:
   There was a wizard from the **west**,
   Whose magic spells were not the **best**.
   He shouted "**Jellyboo**, **kazoodles**!"
   To conjure up a bowl of **noodles**.
   But instead, his favourite **hat**
   Turned into a stripy **cat**.

E3WW21